Contents

Written by
Dennis Hamley
and David Grant

Illustrated by
Mark Boardman

Series editor **Dee Reid**

Heinemann

Part of Pearson

Characters

Tyler

Jack

Tricky words

- dodgems
- prove
- teased
- laughter
- thought
- straight
- desperate
- remembered

Read these words to the student. Help them with these words when they appear in the text.

Introduction

Tyler couldn't wait to get to the fair and go on the rides. He met a boy called Jack and they went on the dodgems together. Then Jack suggested they went on the ghost train. Tyler was scared of ghost trains. He'd been told a story about a boy who had gone missing at a fair 30 years ago. Tyler didn't want Jack to know he was scared, so he went on the ghost train with Jack.

Ghost Ride

Tyler couldn't wait for school to finish.
The fair had set up in the park.
As soon as the bell went, Tyler ran out of school.
"See you all there," he said to his mates.

Tyler got to the park before any of his mates.
He couldn't wait to go on the rides.
He saw a boy standing by the dodgems.
"Want to go on the dodgems with me?" said Tyler.
"OK," said the boy. "My name's Jack."
"I'm Tyler," said Tyler.

They went on loads of rides.
Then, Tyler saw a ride they hadn't been on,
hidden away in a dark corner.
"That's the ghost train!" said Jack. "Let's go on it!"
"Ghost trains are rubbish!" said Tyler.

But really Tyler was scared of ghost trains.
He'd been told a story about a boy who had
gone missing at a fair 30 years ago.
The last place he had been seen was going
into the ghost train.

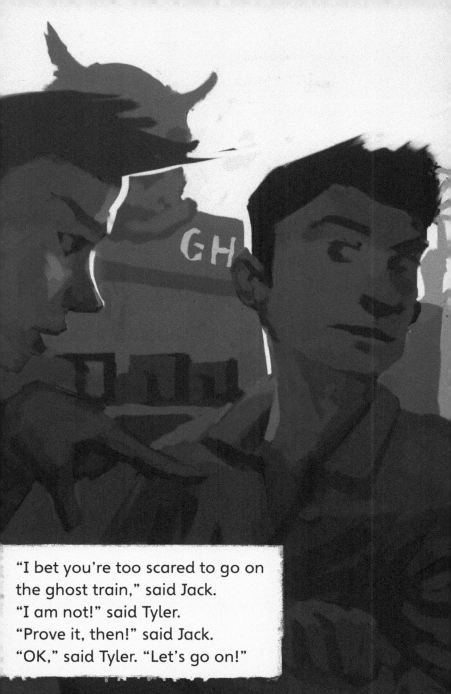

"I bet you're too scared to go on
the ghost train," said Jack.
"I am not!" said Tyler.
"Prove it, then!" said Jack.
"OK," said Tyler. "Let's go on!"

Tyler and Jack got into a cart.
It started moving.
"Try not to scream!" teased Jack.
It was very dark. Tyler and Jack
couldn't see.

Suddenly a ghost jumped out at them.
Tyler jumped, then he laughed.
"Is that meant to be scary?" he said.
"It's just a dummy!"

Then suddenly the cart stopped.
It had turned very cold.
They could no longer hear the sounds of
music and laughter from the fair outside.

Something isn't right, thought Tyler.
He grabbed Jack's arm.
His hand went straight through where
Jack's arm should have been.
He turned to look at Jack.
He could see right through him!

Jack smiled an evil smile.
"You shouldn't have got on the ghost train,"
he said. "You know what happens to boys who
go on the ghost train. They never get off."

Tyler screamed.
He tried to get out of the cart but he couldn't.
He was stuck.
"Help!" he screamed. "Let me out!"
Jack laughed an evil laugh.

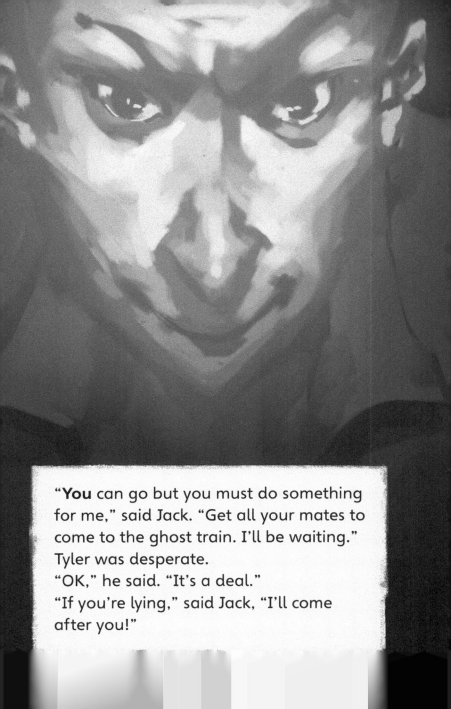

"**You** can go but you must do something for me," said Jack. "Get all your mates to come to the ghost train. I'll be waiting."

Tyler was desperate.

"OK," he said. "It's a deal."

"If you're lying," said Jack, "I'll come after you!"

Suddenly the cart started moving.
In a moment, Tyler was out in the bright sunshine.
He turned to speak to Jack but
there was no sign of him.

Tyler remembered the story about the boy
who went missing at the fair 30 years ago.
What if it had almost happened again?

Tyler ran home.
He looked up the story of the
missing boy on the Internet.
He opened a link to a local newspaper.
It was dated 18 November, 1981.
The headline read 'Local boy missing'.

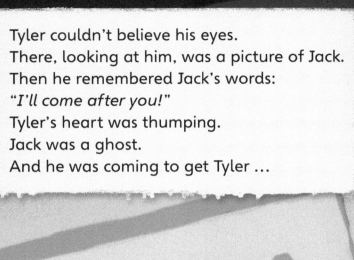

Tyler couldn't believe his eyes.
There, looking at him, was a picture of Jack.
Then he remembered Jack's words:
"I'll come after you!"
Tyler's heart was thumping.
Jack was a ghost.
And he was coming to get Tyler ...

Quiz

Text comprehension

Literal comprehension
p4 What ride did Tyler and Jack go on first?
p6 Why didn't Tyler want to go on the ghost train?

Inferential comprehension
p7 Why does Tyler agree to go on the ghost train with Jack?
p9 Why did Tyler laugh?
p13 Why does Tyler agree to get his mates to go on the ghost train?

Personal response
- Do you think Tyler will get his mates to go on the ghost train?
- What do you think will happen if they do?

Word knowledge

p6 Find a phrase that means 'disappeared'.
p12 Find an adjective used twice on this page.
p16 Which phrase reveals that Tyler was feeling nervous?

Spelling challenge

Read these words:

started   believe   stopped

Now try to spell them!

Ha! Ha! Ha!

What do ghosts like to ride on at the fairground?

The Roller Ghoaster!

Find out about

- the Fox sisters, who said they could speak to spirits and the children of Borley Rectory, who pretended their house was haunted.

Tricky words

- haunted
- murdered
- answer
- neighbours
- hoax
- knuckles
- poltergeist
- wondered

Read these words to the student. Help them with these words when they appear in the text

Introduction

Margaret and Katy Fox were sisters who lived in America in the 1840s. They pretended they could talk to spirits and their mother believed them. But it was all a hoax.
The Bull family said there were ghosts and poltergeists in their house, but later it turned out that it too was a hoax.

HOAXERS

The Fox Sisters

Margaret and Katy Fox were sisters who lived in America in the 1840s. Margaret was 15 and Katy was 11. Their mother was very scared. She said that she heard strange tapping noises at night. Then she heard footsteps.

Margaret and Katy told their mother that the house was haunted.
They said it was the ghost of a man who had been murdered in the house.
They said they could talk to the spirit and it would answer by tapping.

Their mother asked the spirit how many
children she had. The spirit tapped out
its answer. The spirit got the answer right.
Their mother asked the spirit how old her
children were. The spirit knocked again.
It got each answer right. Their mother
asked the neighbours to come and see.
The spirit answered all their questions too.

Margaret and Katy became famous for talking to spirits. Soon they were appearing in shows all over America. Thousands of people paid to see the sisters talk to loved ones and friends who had died.

40 years later, Margaret owned up. She said it was all a hoax.
She and Katy had lied about being able to talk to ghosts. They had made the strange noises in their house by dropping apples on the floor. They had made the tapping noises by secretly cracking the knuckles of their fingers.

The Fox sisters made lots of money by pretending they could talk to spirits. But after Margaret owned up that it was all a hoax, no-one came to their shows any more.

Borley Rectory

Borley Rectory was said to be the most haunted house in Britain. Harry Bull and his 14 children lived there.

The Bull family said that a ghost played the piano in their house. They said that a poltergeist made books fly across the room. They said the ghost of a headless monk walked across the garden.

Hundreds of people came to Borley Rectory hoping to see a real ghost.

Borley Rectory burnt down in 1939.
60 years later, a friend of the Bull family
explained that it had all been a hoax.

He said that the ghost who played the piano was really one of the children. A small boy would lean through a gap in the wall behind the piano and hit the piano strings with a poker.

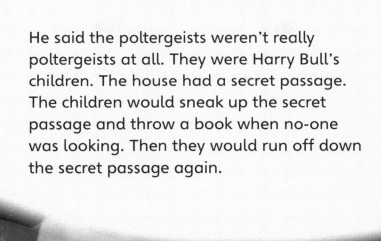

He said the poltergeists weren't really poltergeists at all. They were Harry Bull's children. The house had a secret passage. The children would sneak up the secret passage and throw a book when no-one was looking. Then they would run off down the secret passage again.

The headless monk was not a ghost either.
He was a friend of the family.
Whenever people came to the Rectory
hoping to see a ghost, he would put on a
black cape with the collar turned up.
Then he would slowly walk through the
gardens just as it was getting dark.

Harry Bull's children said they had seen the ghost of a nun who had died 300 years earlier. Some people wondered why it had taken 300 years for the ghost to appear.
Now we know why.
It was because the nun and all the other ghosts were never there at all.

Quiz

Text comprehension

Literal comprehension
p23 Could the Fox sisters really talk to the spirits?
p30 Who was the headless monk?

Inferential comprehension
p21 How were the Fox sisters clever?
p26 Why do you think the Bull children wanted to trick visitors?
p31 What was suspicious about the ghost of the nun?

Personal response
- Do you believe in ghosts?
- Would you have been fooled by the tricks of the Fox sisters or the Bull children?

Word knowledge
p19 Find a word meaning 'mysterious'.
p22 What does the phrase 'loved ones' mean?
p23 Find an adverb in the final sentence.

Spelling challenge
Read these words:
later   children   almost
Now try to spell them!

Ha! Ha! Ha!

Why are ghosts cowards?
Because they have got no guts!